First World War
and Army of Occupation
War Diary
France, Belgium and Germany

37 DIVISION
63 Infantry Brigade,
Brigade Trench Mortar Battery
1 July 1916 - 30 September 1916

WO95/2529/5

The Naval & Military Press Ltd
www.nmarchive.com
Published in association with The National Archives

Published by

The Naval & Military Press Ltd

Unit 10 Ridgewood Industrial Park,

Uckfield, East Sussex,

TN22 5QE England

Tel: +44 (0) 1825 749494

www.naval-military-press.com

www.nmarchive.com

This diary has been reprinted in facsimile from the original. Any imperfections are inevitably reproduced and the quality may fall short of modern type and cartographic standards.

© Crown Copyright
Images reproduced by permission of The National Archives, London, England, 2015.

Contents

Document type	Place/Title	Date From	Date To
Heading	WO95/2529/5		
Heading	Reference WO95 2529 63rd Trench Mortar Battery July-Sep 1916 Conservation Department 11-3-1999		
Heading	37th Division 63rd Infy Bde 63rd Trench Mortar Bty Jly-Sep 1916		
War Diary	Fricourt	01/07/1916	04/07/1916
War Diary	Vaux	08/07/1916	08/07/1916
War Diary	Grenas	11/07/1918	11/07/1918
War Diary	Bienvillers	14/07/1918	18/07/1918
War Diary	Gouy-Servins	18/07/1918	25/07/1918
War Diary	Berthonval	26/07/1916	13/08/1916
War Diary	Dieval	23/07/1916	24/07/1916
War Diary	La Coupe	24/08/1916	31/08/1916
War Diary		29/08/1918	29/08/1918
War Diary	37th Division. Q.	04/09/1916	04/09/1916
War Diary	La Compte	01/09/1916	30/09/1916

REFERENCE

**WO
95**

2529

**63rd TRENCH
MORTAR BATTERY
JULY – SEP 1916**

CONSERVATION DEPARTMENT

11-3-1999

37TH DIVISION
63RD INFY BDE

63RD TRENCH MORTAR BTY

JLY - SEP 1916

63rd T.M Bty

Army Form C. 2118

WAR DIARY
or
INTELLIGENCE SUMMARY

(Erase heading not required.)

Place	Date	Hour	Summary of Events and Information	Remarks and references to Appendices
Fricourt	Sept 1st		The Battery took part in preliminary bombardment and to Battery supported infantry in attack on German front line. The Battery losing 2 officers (Lieut Johnston – 2nd (Rimington) + 16 O.R. in the attack. The Battery Sgt. (Sgt Westbrook) re-organized the men + took up a position in German front line, where great work was done in support of infantry.	J4. Sep '16
"	Sept 2nd		Acted as reserve for 63rd Brigade.	
"	" 3		Acted as ammunition carrying party for 62nd Brigade + later at night were relieved + marched from Trenches.	
Vaux	" 4		Proceeded to Beaucourt + entrained, arriving at Vaux that evening	
"	" 8		Resting + refitting	
Gremes	" 11		Training to complete establishment	
"	11		Left Gremes for Trenches. (Beaumettes)	
Bainvillers	" 11		Trenches	
"	13		The 20th M of 13th West took a discharge of Gas + at intervals, an	

WAR DIARY or INTELLIGENCE SUMMARY

Army Form C. 2118

Place	Date	Hour	Summary of Events and Information	Remarks and references to Appendices
Bruilles	13th		Artillery bombardment, in supporting an attack by 4th Army, on our right. The Battn. was instructed to stand by, but were not required.	
	14th	4 P.M.	Paraded at 4 P.M. & marched to Humbercamp.	
	15th		Marched to Houvin	
	16th		Marched to Challon	
	17th		Resting	
	18th		Marched to Gouy-Servins. During these marches our transport proved our unsatisfaction, we had great difficulty in keeping up with the Brigade.	
Gouy-Servins	19th to 25th		Training	
	25th		Left Gouy-Servins for Trenches	
Berthonval	26th to 31st		In Trenches. During this visit to Trenches, the Battn. did good work in constructing work started on emplacements, also great improvement dug-out accommodation. A large number of names were expended in retaliation. The enemy being at times very offensive, & rumour were sent out and took effect. Working parties were also found	

1875 Wt. W593/826 1,000,000 4/15 J.B.C. & A. A.D.S.S./Forms/C.2118.

Army Form C. 2118

63rd Trench Mortar Battery Vol 2

WAR DIARY
or
INTELLIGENCE SUMMARY
(Erase heading not required.)

Instructions regarding War Diaries and Intelligence Summaries are contained in F.S. Regs., Part II. and the Staff Manual respectively. Title Pages will be prepared in manuscript.

Place	Date	Hour	Summary of Events and Information	Remarks and references to Appendices
Bethonsart	Aug 1		Trenches. Time was well employed in work on emplacements = dug-outs, & immediate number of rounds were fired in retaliation	
	" 12		Left Trenches for Souy-Servin	
	" 12		Marched to Dieval. A very long + tiring march. (transport again from us unsatisfactory)	
Dieval	" 13		Training	
	23		Marched to Souy-Servin	
La Comté	24		Attached to 9th Tr. Training own storming Trenches	
	31		G.O.C. 1st Army Inspection	
	31		Lieut O'Kieman took over command of Battery from 2nd Lt Edwards	
	29		2nd Lt Harris + 2nd Lt Trapham also joined	
			2nd Lt Edwards & 2nd Lt Andreus rejoined their Batts	

37th Division. Q.

> 63RD INFANTRY BRIGADE.
> No. 8961
> Date 4/9/16

Herewith August War Diary of the 63rd Trench Mortar Battery.

4/9/16.

L. Morris Captain
Brigade Major
63rd Infantry Bde.

WAR DIARY
or
INTELLIGENCE SUMMARY
(Erase heading not required.)

Army Form C. 2118

63 Trench Mortar Batty

Vol 3

Place	Date	Hour	Summary of Events and Information	Remarks and references to Appendices
La Boiselle	Sept 2		Tommy at La Boiselle attacked to g[un] Devision.	
	11th		Left La Boiselle marched to gun demonstration — Officers received have opened influenza	
	12th		Battery left going down for intensive (Von Gogh) training given to take part in line by the Germans. The British made very heavy during the	
	13th		fire. The enforcement were used in British and greatest Guns were seen in enormous numbers. In some cases are	
	14		three guns in a salvo appeared. Above all the he were also employed in delivering shells. The new model of French army this far day and by the evening of the 14th or haveticm were in order and ammunition received at Augmn. had inaugurated an enemy bombardment. The my began 14th The Main had flown. The Battery had 8 guns in a line an front of 50 gds. Zero was at 10.7 pm. Each gun fired at Zero and 2 min — every four sec at rate of 20 rounds he.	

WAR DIARY or INTELLIGENCE SUMMARY

Army Form C. 2118

63 Trench Mortar Battery

Place	Date	Hour	Summary of Events and Information	Remarks and references to Appendices
	Sept 14		minute. The My arty by Battery (4 guns) commenced at zero hour about + 7 minute. The left half Battery + gun fired 90 Jps at + 2 minute. All eight guns fired during the firsts & onwards homch about 7 minute the night ½ Battery also fired 90 Jps firing at same rate. The whole Battery commenced on the spot fire plan having + 3 minute; at + 30 minute Battery advance 90 Jps and went + 32 advance further firing at same rate. All the guns answered very few misfiring. Even the French made the guns were very hot Sometimes in some cases even burnt through. The roof the Battery dutson on the two day however the guns never had trouble at times a perfect barrage of shrapnel + H.E. was come lucky to have escaped without casualties. The raid was a great success. Th morning there was movement on front sm	

63 Trench Mortar Battery

Army Form C. 2118

WAR DIARY
or
INTELLIGENCE SUMMARY
(Erase heading not required.)

Instructions regarding War Diaries and Intelligence Summaries are contained in F.S. Regs., Part II. and the Staff Manual respectively. Title Pages will be prepared in manuscript.

Place	Date	Hour	Summary of Events and Information	Remarks and references to Appendices
	Sept 15		About 3.5 about 9 a.m. were rested in the front his alone, in about 2 may have used of our fashion when you suffer. The enemy, hastly suffered a drive measuring the "cookers" hummy was as average a day worker there later manoeuvres. The men attended anywhere cut orders with site about of things	
	16		Left trenches at 7:30 a.m. and went for 9 to 10 doesn't and eigenal	
	18		6.3 wt. top Bergard the hit	
			Left Going done at 9 a.m. for two howitz 1/2 Battery into trenches Sunday I.2	
	22 23		11/2 yrs half Battery relieved left half Battery Working parties and refreshments also working in new explosives	
	26 30		some fired during the two men along in trenches one or others three hundred.	

J. Akerman
Capt. 6663 T.M.B.